Glazed

Amina Ali

Presentation by *BookLeaf Publishing*

Web: www.bookleafpub.com

E-mail: info@bookleafpub.com

ISBN: 9789358369625

First edition 2023

DEDICATION

To Mom and Dad,

This book is dedicated to both of you, my pillars of support and love. You have given me the greatest gift of all - the life and opportunity to explore, learn, and grow. Your unwavering belief in me has nurtured my dreams and shaped the person I have become. Thank you for guiding me through the highs and lows, always providing a steady hand and a loving heart. This dedication is a testament to your endless love and sacrifices, which have allowed me to chase my own experiences and create a life filled with purpose and fulfillment.

To my dear friends,

This dedication is also for you, my cherished companions who have walked alongside me on this incredible journey. Your presence has kept me on my toes, challenging me to push beyond my limits and discover new horizons. Your unwavering support, laughter, and shared adventures have enriched my life in countless ways. Together, we have created memories that will forever be etched in my heart. Thank you for being my confidants, my partners in crime, and the ones who continually inspire me to embrace life's possibilities.

To my parents and friends, your love, encouragement, and unwavering presence have shaped my story. This book is a tribute to your profound impact on my life, and I am forever grateful for the profound love and support you have provided.

With the deepest gratitude,

Amina

PREFACE

To my dear readers,

As you embark on this literary voyage, I want you to know that we are not mere strangers, but fellow travelers on this extraordinary journey called life. Together, we will share moments of unbridled joy and inconsolable pain, for our connection goes beyond the pages of this book.

Within these words, I lay bare my vulnerabilities and triumphs, inviting you to join me in laughter, tears, and the occasional misstep. Through our shared experiences, we will discover solace in the knowledge that we are never truly alone.

In penning these pages, I am eager to express my unwavering optimism, a beacon of light that illuminates even the darkest corners. Life's unpredictable twists and turns hold no power over us, for we are ready to face them head-on, armed with resilience and hope.

It is with profound gratitude that I embark on this journey with you, my cherished audience. Your presence lends meaning to my words, transforming them into a bridge that connects souls and ignites collective strength.

Together, let us embrace the boundless possibilities that lie ahead and celebrate the beauty that emerges from the interplay of triumph and adversity.

With heartfelt appreciation,

Amina Ali

22

To only live once, society claims,
A mantra forced down our weary throats,
But as we strive to forge our own names,
We yearn to be stars in the sky that floats.

Oh, the twisted joy of this constant spiral,
Emotions swirling, never finding rest,
The world often shrugs when our fire turns frail,
Unaware of the burdens within our chest.

We smile, though rivers of tears overflow,
Hiding our pain behind a mask of glee,
To only live once, we're told to show,
But what of the depth within, can they see?

Making memories becomes a tiresome chore,
Appreciated merely for their polished sheen,
The euphoria they bring fades, alas, and more,
Vanishing swiftly as if it were a dream.

To only live once, they say, without crime,
Yet shackled by their guidelines, we're confined,
If we fail to fit their mold, their paradigm,
The world turns its back, leaving us behind.

But listen, young heart, hear my whispered plea,

Amidst the cacophony of societal noise,
Embrace your truth, let your spirit roam free,
Seek the path that resonates with your voice.

For to only live once is a sacred gift,
A chance to dance upon this earthly stage,
Don't let their expectations cause your spirit to
shift,
Unleash your essence, unleash your rage.

Break free from the chains that hold you tight,
Embrace the wild, uncharted unknown,
For it's in the pursuit of your own light,
That your authentic self will truly be shown.

So, defy their norms, their shallow demands,
Forge your own path, in every twist and bend,
Live fiercely, love passionately, take a stance,
For this is the chance, the one life you'll spend.

And remember, dear soul, as you journey on,
Amidst the challenges society imposes,
To only live once is not just a con,
It's an opportunity to break free from those
shackles.

Narcissist

I could start with the word narcissist,
And no, it's not about me,
It's about you, the captor of souls,
The master of manipulation, I see.

What does it feel like to constantly gaslight,
To twist the truth and hide your lies?
To feed on the vulnerability of another,
Leaving them shattered, struggling to rise?

You reveled in your self-created power,
Binding hearts with your deceitful chains,
But I've emerged, breaking free at last,
From the depths where darkness still remains.

I shed the shackles that held me tight,
And rediscovered my own worth and grace,
No longer a prisoner of your false charms,
I'm reclaiming my life, my sacred space.

I found strength in the depths of despair,
Gathering fragments of a broken soul,
Piece by piece, I stitched myself anew,
Embracing healing, making myself whole.

I refused to let your toxicity define me,
For I am resilient, I am unbreakable,
I turned my pain into a beacon of light,
A testament to the human spirit, unstoppable.

In the wake of your narcissistic storm,
I found solace in my own authenticity,
Learning to love and trust myself once more,
Releasing the burden, setting my spirit free.

So, here I stand, a survivor, a warrior,
Having triumphed over your twisted game,
No longer a victim to your manipulation,
For I have emerged, forever changed.

I rise above the ashes of our broken past,
Leaving behind the shadows that once loomed,
With newfound strength, I reclaim my voice,
A testament to the power of being exhumed.

So, dear narcissist, this is not your story,
It's a tale of resilience, of rising above,
From the embers of pain, I found my voice,
And now, I soar on wings of self-love.

In the realm of healing and self-discovery,
I found the power to break free,
No longer confined by your toxic grasp,
I've overcome your narcissistic legacy.

White Noise

I can hear the static in my head,
The disarray that fills the empty space,
Concentration eludes me, thoughts widespread,
Lost in the chaos, a restless chase.

Amidst the clamor, a symphony of sound,
The white noise engulfs my weary soul,
But within its depths, solace is found,
A gateway to peace, my ultimate goal.

In the midst of obligations, tasks galore,
My mind struggles to find a focal point,
But the white noise hums, a comforting lore,
Guiding me towards a tranquil joint.

Like a gentle breeze, it whispers serenity,
Through the discordant echoes in my mind,
Melting away the layers of anxiety,
Revealing a stillness, so hard to find.

I surrender to the white noise's embrace,
Letting its soothing tendrils entwine,
As it carries me to a sacred space,
Where the cluttered thoughts can align.

Within its static, I discover clarity,
A refuge from the demands that surround,
The white noise becomes my sanctuary,
Where tranquility and purpose are found.

So, I embrace the symphony within,
And let the white noise weave its spell,
For amidst the chaos, peace begins,
A sanctuary where my spirit can dwell.

In this dance of thoughts and sounds,
I find a rhythm that sets me free,
The white noise, a guide when anxiety abounds,
Leading me to a state of inner harmony.

Though the world may buzz with ceaseless
noise,
I can find solace in the white noise's art,
With its gentle whispers, it brings me poise,
A connection to peace that mends my heart.

Blackberry

Today was rather tart,
It wasn't a bad day, but it could've been better.
Like a blackberry, sweet and sharp,
I carried the highs and lows on my shoulders.

In the morning's embrace, I tasted the sun,
Its warmth spreading through my veins,
But as the hours passed, clouds begun
To cast shadows, stirring subtle strains.

Just like a blackberry, with its vibrant hue,
I navigated through today's twists and turns,
Each moment a mixture of joy and rue,
As today's lessons unfold, my heart yearns.

Sometimes today's sweetness enveloped my
soul,
Juicy moments of laughter and delight,
But other times, like thorny patches took their
toll,
Pricking my spirit, causing inner fight.

Yet, within the blackberry's complex taste,
I find solace in today's intricate blend,
For it's in the contrast I've come to embrace,

That I discover my strength and mend.

So, as the day wanes and darkness seeps,
I'll hold onto hope, amidst the storm's sway,
Knowing that tomorrow, the sun still peeps,
Another chance to savor life's blackberry array.

For in its tangy tartness lies my truth,
A reminder that life's flavors intertwine,
And though today may be bittersweet, uncouth,
I'll savor it all, for it's truly mine.

11:11

A sign to keep going has presented itself to me,
A gentle nudge in the midst of uncertainty,
At a time when I needed it the most,
A beacon of guidance, a comforting host.

This is the start to a new chapter in my life,
A blank page ready to be filled with delight,
Every experience, every challenge I've faced,
Has shaped my journey, has left its trace.

Any struggles up to this point were preparing me
for now,
Each obstacle overcome, a lesson to endow,
Strength and resilience have grown within,
Equipping me for the path I'm about to begin.

All accomplishments were just the start,
Building the foundation, igniting a spark,
To pave the way for myself, to discover and
explore,
Unveiling the potential I've yet to explore.

As I turn the page and embrace the unknown,
I carry with me the wisdom I've sown,
The past has shaped me, but it doesn't define me,

The boundless possibilities that now align.

So, with gratitude and anticipation in my heart,
I step into this new chapter, ready to chart,
A journey filled with growth, love, and grace,
Embracing the future, with a smile on my face.

Welcome to the End

Often times I think that the end,
A concept that unsettles, makes me apprehend,
But deep within, I've come to comprehend,
That the end doesn't signify a permanent
descend.

For in every finale, a new chapter emerges,
A chance for growth, where resilience surges,
The end becomes a threshold, a gateway,
Welcoming me to a vibrant array.

So, welcome to the end, where possibilities
thrive,
A moment to bid farewell, and then to arrive,
To release the past, with its weight and strain,
Embracing the future, unburdened by the chain.

The end is not an abyss of despair,
But a catalyst for change, a breath of fresh air,
It signifies the closing of one beautiful tale,
And opens the curtains for the next to prevail.

In each ending lies the seeds of beginnings,
Opportunities awaiting, like whispered inklings,
The end is where transformation can ignite,

A chance to soar and bask in a newfound light.

So I choose not to dwell on what's left behind,
Instead, I embrace the end, with a hopeful mind,
For it's in these closures that I truly find,
The strength to let go and leave the past behind.

Welcome to the end, where hope takes flight,
Where the old dissolves, and the new shines
bright,
With every conclusion, a fresh journey begins,
A chance to grow, as life gracefully spins.

Make The Days

365 days we have,
A tapestry of moments waiting to be embraced,
Within the time we have in the day,
Choice lies within, where destinies are traced.

You can either make the grass greener,
With every step you take, nurturing its hue,
Or ponder on why the cup is half empty,
While the world around you continues to accrue.

The dawn whispers secrets of possibilities,
As the sun rises with its gentle kiss,
Painting the canvas of the day with golden hues,
Inviting you to step into the abyss.

Time is but a fleeting companion,
Yet within its grasp, magic resides,
For every second holds the power,
To shape the path where passion resides.

In the tapestry of hours unfurling,
Lies the choice to breathe life into dreams,
To seize the day with purpose and intention,
And bathe in the sunlight's radiant beams.

The clock ticks with rhythmic certainty,
Each moment a chance to redefine,
Will you let worries weigh you down,
Or let your spirit gracefully align?

Within the bounds of the fleeting day,
You hold the key to ignite the flame,
To savor every morsel of existence,
And make the days truly your own name.

So, choose to fill the hours with joy,
Inscribe laughter upon the moments you find,
Embrace the gift of time's abundance,
And leave no trace of regret behind.

365 days we have, a tapestry we weave,
With every breath, a chance to create,
Choose the type of day you're going to have,
For within your hands, there's always enough
time.
For within the span of each passing day,
Lies the power to mend and to mend anew,
To live with gratitude and an open heart,
And let your dreams guide the choices you
pursue.

So, make the days a symphony of moments,
Tune each note with love and delight,
For within the tapestry of 365 days,

You have the power to make each one shine
bright.

And It's Over.

To think I spent hours
Entwined in a web of regrets and doubts,
Tangled in the threads of what could have been,
Lost in the labyrinth of my own thoughts.

Repeating scenes of the past and future,
As if replaying them would change the outcome,
But the truth finally breaks through the haze,
This constant rumination is nothing but a prison.

Pondering over the how and why,
Searching for answers that will never come,
But now I see the futility of it all,
For the past is etched in stone, never to be
undone.

My eyes want to burn in red,
From tears shed over illusions and shattered
dreams,
But they will dry, and clarity will replace the
pain,
For healing starts when acceptance gleams.

From the storm that's ready,
To glaze across them in tempestuous wrath,

I will emerge, stronger and wiser than before,
For I have found solace in my own chosen path.

But I now understand this is a temporary feeling,
A passing storm that obscures my inner light,
For I am not defined by your absence or
presence,
I am the brilliance that shines even in the darkest
night.

And it's over, this chapter finally closed,
The curtain falls, and a new act begins,
Tomorrow, I'll be back to being me,
Unburdened, unfettered, ready to spread my
wings.

Unbothered and untouched by your evil energy,
I rise above the toxicity, reclaiming my power,
No longer entangled in what might have been,
For my spirit soars, reaching heights that tower.

So, I leave you behind, with grace and a smile,
Knowing that my worth cannot be confined,
I outshine the shadows you tried to cast,
For I am the embodiment of strength, redefined.

In this journey of self-discovery and growth,
I reclaim my joy, my freedom, and my peace,
No longer haunted by the past's ghost,

I emerge victorious, finding sweet release.

For I am back to being myself, shining bright,
No longer burdened by thoughts that weigh me
down,
And as I move forward, leaving you in my wake,
I know my true worth will always outshine your
crown.

Myself & Kin

I project myself into those around me,
My brothers and sisters, a cherished family,
For they hold a piece of my very essence,
And I yearn to ignite their inner brilliance.

I want to inspire not just blood, but all,
To embrace my creativity and compassion's call,
To share the humble flare that burns within,
And spread the light, erasing shadows so thin.

I see reflections of myself in their eyes,
The connections they forge, the dreams they
devise,
Together, we navigate life's winding road,
Unyielding to negativity's heavy load.

No envious clans or negative strife,
Shall deter them from the path of a meaningful
life,
I stand as their guardian, their guiding star,
Protecting their spirits from distances afar.

For one day, it may just be us, kin alone,
But in that unity, a love deeply grown,
And in that moment, we'll realize with pride,

That strength lies in the bond we confide.

Is it truly a bad thing, this destiny we share?
No, for within our unity, love fills the air,
I wouldn't want it any other way,
Together, we'll illuminate the darkest day.

So, I aspire to inspire them with my light,
To ignite a flame that will forever burn bright,
To show them the depths of their own worth,
And empower them to conquer the earth.

May they see in me a source of motivation,
A reminder of the limitless potential of their
creation,
With every step they take, the extra mile,
I'll be there, cheering them on with a smile.

Together, we'll radiate as a golden light,
Guiding others towards their own lofty height,
For the future rests in their hands, it's true,
And through positive energy,
They'll push on and breakthrough.
So, let me be a beacon of hope and delight,
A reminder that they have the power to ignite,
The world awaits, ready to be transformed,
And with inspiration as our guide, we'll perform.

We'll paint vibrant colors on life's canvas,

Embracing diversity, for it is our essence,
Unleashing passions, talents, and dreams,
Creating a tapestry woven with endless themes.

With every step they take, I'll be their guide,
Nurturing their spirits, standing by their side,
Encouraging courage when doubts arise,
Instilling in them the belief to reach the skies.

I'll share stories of triumph, resilience, and
grace,
Of individuals who dared to find their place,
In the face of adversity, they persevered,
Their strength and determination revered.

And as they grow, they'll realize their might,
A force of change, radiating pure light,
Their impact expanding far and wide,
A testament to the power they hold inside.

For the future is shaped by hearts that care,
By those who believe that love will repair,
The fractures in our world, the tears and strife,
With empathy and compassion as their guiding
life.

I'll be there to celebrate every victory,
To lend a hand during moments of uncertainty,
Together, we'll uplift and inspire,

Fueling the flames of passion, burning brighter
and higher.

And when the time comes for me to depart,
I'll leave behind a legacy in each heart,
A legacy of inspiration and profound love,
A reminder of the limitless heights they're
capable of.

So, let us embark on this journey, hand in hand,
Spreading positive energy throughout the land,
Empowering others to embrace their unique
voice,
For together, we'll make the world rejoice.

My siblings, my kin, and all who cross my way,
May my light guide you to a brighter day,
Know that within you lies a boundless fire,
And through inspiration, you'll continue to
inspire.

Glazed

I have this habit of glazing over my emotions,
Hiding them beneath a mask, a delicate potion,
The things that bring me joy, fleetingly pass,
While the sorrows linger, like shards of glass.

But behind the smile I carefully adorn,
Lies a truth, a struggle that is yet unborn,
To be numb to my own feelings, I confess,
A tangled web of confusion, I must address.

I sense something amiss, a whisper in my core,
Yet acknowledging the truth, I dare no more,
For to face the depths of my inner sea,
Takes courage and vulnerability.

But within this struggle, I'll find my way,
Unraveling the knots that hold dismay,
For ignoring my own emotions won't make them
cease,
They linger like echoes, seeking release.

I'll navigate the labyrinth of my own mind,
With patience and compassion, I'll gently
unwind,
Each emotion, a thread to be explored,

Acknowledging their presence, not to be
ignored.

I'll create a sanctuary, a safe space to feel,
Where my emotions are welcomed, genuine and
real,
For it's in their embrace, I'll truly understand,
The beauty and complexity of who I am.

No longer will I fear the waves that crash,
I'll ride them bravely, with resilience and
panache,
With each rise and fall, I'll grow stronger still,
Embracing the full spectrum, no longer standing
still.

For in acknowledging my emotions, I find,
A deeper connection to the depths of
humankind,
And through this journey of self-discovery,
I'll uncover the answers, the keys to set me free.

I'll no longer be glazed,
But instead, embrace them with heartfelt
devotion,
For in their whispers and cries, I'll discover the
truth,
And in that vulnerability, I'll find my own
verity's root.

Mirrored

It's okay to sometimes see in the mirror's
reflection,
A version of me with an altered complexion,
She stands before me, claiming to be my ego,
A side of myself that I've come to know.

In her eyes, a confidence shines bright,
A self-assuredness that challenges the night,
She whispers, whispers of ambition and pride,
Urge me to conquer, to stride fiercely.

But within her presence, I tread with care,
For ego's allure can lead me unaware,
I pause to ponder the intentions behind it,
To navigate this realm, both gentle and kind.

For ego can blind, its vanity sway,
But in balance, it offers a unique display,
A reminder of my worth, a sense of esteem,
Yet humility's grace must remain on my team.

So, I embrace this apparition I see,
My ego's reflection, a part of me,
But I tread the path with self-awareness in tow,
Guided by authenticity's gentle glow.

I'll honor my achievements, embrace my power,
Yet humbly acknowledge each passing hour,
For ego's voice can be both boon and bane,
A delicate dance to keep it restrained.

In the mirror's gaze, I find clarity,
The wisdom to navigate the ego's duality,
To nurture self-confidence, let it bloom,
But never at the expense of compassion's room.

For true growth lies not in ego's sway,
But in the connections, I forge, day by day,
To uplift others, to lend a helping hand,
To build a world where empathy expands.

So, as I stand before this mirrored reflection,
I'll heed the call to introspection,
Embrace my ego's presence, yet remain aware,
To channel its energy with mindful care.

In the dance of self-discovery, I'll find,
A harmony where ego and spirit intertwine,
And through this journey, I'll strive to be,
A reflection of authenticity, shining free.

Have You

Have you ever lost a laugh that was so pure,
A melody of joy that will no longer endure,
Its echoes fade, carried on the wind's gentle sigh,
Leaving an emptiness, a tear in the sky.

Have you ever lost a smile that was so bright,
Radiating warmth, like a beacon of light,
Its absence leaves a void, a shadowed space,
A memory held tightly, within the heart's
embrace.

Have you ever lost a friend that was so special,
A bond unbreakable, a connection celestial,
Their presence is etched deeply, within your
soul,
Their absence is a reminder of the stories untold.

The pain of loss weighs heavy on our hearts,
Aching with the longing for a fresh new start,
But as we navigate through grief's winding
course,
We find solace in memories, a healing force.

In moments of silence, we'll hear their voice,
Whispering love, reminding us of choice,

To honor their spirit, their light that shone,
We'll carry their essence, never truly alone.

Though they may have departed from this
earthly plane,
Their love remains, an eternal flame,
We cherish the laughter, the smiles they
bestowed,
Keeping their spirit alive, a vibrant ode.

And as time passes, the ache may subside,
Replaced by gratitude for the joy that did reside,
In the moments shared, the love that was pure,
Their essence forever in our hearts, secure.

So, let us remember the laughs and the smiles,
The friendship that graced our lives for a while,
For even in loss, their impact remains,
A testament to the love that forever sustains.

Chromatic Smiles

No one truly knows the depth that lies within,
Behind my chromatic smiles, where emotions
begin,
A spectrum of expressions, each with its own
hue,
Revealing fragments of the heart, both old and
new.

Some smiles are a facade, a mask to wear,
Concealing the storms, the burdens I bear,
Yet others hold secrets, joys untold,
Moments of bliss that words cannot unfold.

My chromatic smiles, they speak in their own
way,
A language of emotions, in colors they portray,
For within each curve, a story lies,
A glimpse into the soul, where truth resides.

There's the smile that radiates pure delight,
A burst of sunshine, a beacon so bright,
It dances with laughter, free and unrestrained,
Unveiling the joy that cannot be contained.

Then there's the smile that conceals the tears,

A shield against the pain, the doubts, and fears,
It whispers strength, a silent battle won,
A resolute spirit that carries on.

And amidst the colors, there's a smile so serene,
A tranquil oasis, where peace is seen,
It emanates calmness, a soothing embrace,
Reflecting the inner tranquility I chase.

But beneath them all, a common thread prevails,
A longing for connection, where authenticity
unveils,
For my chromatic smiles, though diverse they
may be,
All carry a spark, a glimmer of me.

No smile is empty, no emotion in vain,
Each holds a piece of who I am, in its domain,
They paint a canvas of complexities untold,
A kaleidoscope of emotions, stories unfold.

So, behold my chromatic smiles, a tapestry of
my soul,
Expressing the depths within, making me whole,
For within their hues, the truth quietly resides,
My smiles, my essence, a reflection that abides.

Inhale

I often need to remind myself, it's true,
That life's unpredictability can leave me askew,
In those moments when frustration starts to rise,
I need to take a breath and let calmness baptize
me.

Inhale, I whisper, as my lungs expand,
Drawing in the air, a pause I command,
For within that breath, a sacred space is found,
Where clarity emerges, a tranquil ground.

Not everything will go precisely as planned,
But with each breath, I release what's out of
hand,
A gentle reminder that I hold the power,
To navigate the challenges, hour by hour.

It's easy for my eyes to flood, I admit,
To let emotions overwhelm and tightly grip,
But in that breath, I find solace and release,
A chance to gather strength, find inner peace.

As my head fills with steam, thoughts in a whirl,
I turn to the breath, a steady anchor unfurls,
It clears the fog, like a gentle breeze,

Restoring clarity, setting my mind at ease.

Inhale, I remind myself, with each breath I take,
A moment to center, my composure to remake,
To pause and reflect before I react,
And choose my response, with mindfulness
intact.

For in the breath lies a pause, a sacred key,
Unlocking the wisdom deep within me,
So, I embrace the power of this simple act,
To find balance and grace, to tactfully interact.

Inhale, I repeat, as I navigate the tide,
Allowing each breath to be my guide,
To soften my edges, to find a serene flow,
And in that space, a peaceful rhythm will grow.

So, when life's challenges come my way,
I'll remember to breathe, to calmly sway,
For in that breath, lies the strength I seek,
To respond with grace, and find the peace I
keep.

Inhale, I remind myself, with patience and care,
To let go of expectations and release any snare,
For each breath carries a message of surrender,
A reminder that in stillness, I find my center.

With each inhale, I gather my scattered thoughts,
Exhaling out tensions, the battles I've fought,
It's in this rhythm, this dance of breath,
That I find the resilience to face life's breadth.

Inhale, I whisper, as the world spins around,
Finding solace in the silence, a sanctuary I've
found,
For in the space between the inhale and exhale,
I discover the courage to prevail.

With a mindful breath, I cultivate patience and
grace,
Allowing understanding to take its rightful
place,
In the symphony of moments, I find my way,
Embracing the present, come what may.

So, as the storms of life may stir and churn,
I'll anchor myself in the breath, a lesson I've
learned,
Inhale, I'll say, with a gentle smile,
Knowing that each breath will reconcile.

For in the simple act of breathing, I find release,
A moment of pause, where worries cease,
Inhale, I affirm, as I step into the unknown,
Trusting that with each breath, I have grown.

Runner Up

So used to having my eyes on gold,
My hunger for victory, fierce and bold,
Yet here I stand, handed a silver prize,
A bitter taste of anger, I can't disguise.

Isn't enough, this second place I hold,
A searing fire within, my rage unfolds,
I feel scorched on the inside, burning hot,
Angry and indignant, I give it all I've got.

How dare this happen to me, I seethe,
My dreams of triumph dashed, I cannot believe,
I've poured my heart, my soul into this fight,
Only to be left with a feeling of spite.

But in this anger, a flame takes hold,
Fueling my determination, fierce and bold,
I'll channel the fury, the fire within,
To push myself further, to rise and win.

No longer will I settle for the runner-up's crown,
I'll forge my path to conquer and renown,
For anger can ignite a relentless fire,
Driving me forward, higher and higher.

No longer bound by the shackles of defeat,
I'll use this fury as a propulsive heat,
To fuel my ambition, my relentless drive,
And emerge as a champion, fully alive.

So, watch me rise from this simmering rage,
A force to reckon with, a tempest on stage,
For anger may consume, but it also fuels,
Transforming my despair into victorious jewels.

I won't let this setback define my fate,
Anger transforms into a relentless state,
Pushing me beyond what I thought I could be,
A phoenix rising from the ashes, wild and free.

Zero

Infinity comes a long way, stretching beyond the
horizon,
Yet here I stand, feeling far from a soaring
falcon,
Not a 10 in energy, not even close, I confess,
Is it okay to dwell at zero, feeling less and less?

Amidst the sea of vibrant souls, their spirits
ablaze,
I question my own worth, lost in a weary haze,
Is it acceptable to embrace this lackluster state,
To admit my fatigue, my depleted mental
weight?

The world whirls in motion, a relentless pace,
But I find myself at zero, in a tranquil space,
Does it make me inadequate, to be void of
fervor,
To yearn for stillness, a respite from life's
fervor?

In a society that glorifies perpetual motion,
I question if it's alright to choose a slower
notion,
To recharge and rejuvenate, to find my own way,

Without conforming to the pressure, come what
may.

Perhaps it's in these moments, devoid of grand
zest,
That I discover my essence, find peace in my
chest,
For zero is not a failure, nor a sign of defeat,
But a reminder to nurture, to find solace and
retreat.

In the stillness of zero, I unravel and unwind,
Exploring the depths of my own complex mind,
Allowing space for introspection, self-care, and
grace,
Embracing the ebb and flow, finding my own
pace.

So, I'll acknowledge this emptiness, this humble
state,
Recognizing that energy fluctuates, at any rate,
For it's in these moments of zero, I find a
chance,
To recalibrate, to heal, to rise and enhance.

It's okay to feel at zero, to rest and replenish,
To honor the need for stillness, to cherish and
cherish,

For within this quietude, I lay the groundwork
anew,
To bloom once again, with energy vibrant and
true.

So, let me embrace this zero, without judgment
or scorn,
And from its depths, a resilient spirit shall be
reborn,
For in every pause, every moment of tranquil
reprieve,
Lies the potential for growth, the power to
believe.

In the realm of zero, I find a unique grace,
A chance to rediscover, to embrace my own
pace,
It's a sanctuary of quiet, where I can unfold,
Allowing my weary spirit to be gently consoled.

In the absence of exuberance, I search deep
within,
Exploring the depths where my passions have
been,
For zero is not a void, but a canvas pristine,
A space to reimagine and redefine what I've
seen.

It's in these moments of stillness, where wisdom
is found,
A chance to reconnect, to hear my heart's sound,
To listen to the whispers that often go unheard,
And let my soul be nurtured, gently stirred.

Petty Blues

I don't really care, I'll proudly claim my petty
crown,
For when provoked, my wrath will surely come
down,
In subtle ways, I'll make you feel the sting,
Fueling my fire, the petty blues they bring.

Is it something in the air, an invisible force at
play,
That ignites these thoughts, leading me astray?
Call it what you want, a touch of mischief,
perhaps,
I embrace the pettiness, like an unexpected
lapse.

Sometimes I surprise even myself, with the
lengths I'll go,
To retaliate, to let my petty side show,
I must confess, I have a penchant for this game,
Where pride and ego fuel my flames.

But within this realm of pettiness, I find release,
A momentary pleasure, a sense of inner peace,
It may not be noble, nor something to boast,

Yet the petty blues remind me, I'm human at
most.

So let me revel in these petty shades,
Embracing the flaws that my soul cascades,
For even in the depths of my smallest acts,
I learn the lessons, how to mend and impact.

In the grand tapestry of life, petty moments pass,
Leaving room for growth, for wisdom to amass,
I'll strive to rise above, to let empathy reign,
And curb the petty blues, breaking free from its
chain.

For in the end, it's love and kindness that prevail,
As the petty blues, with time, begin to pale,
I'll seek forgiveness and understanding anew,
Shedding the shackles of pettiness, starting
anew.

So, let me acknowledge my petty inclinations,
But also strive for grace and higher vibrations,
In the symphony of life, let compassion play,
And bid farewell to the petty blues, day by day.

My Basket

The sun, my basket,
Guardian of my happiest moments,
Its warm embrace holds my deepest sentiments,
Yet lately, its radiant locks keep me out.

How does it sense my defiance, my attempt to
break free,
My mind overflows with the cries of a heavy
heart,
Seeking solace, I turn to my basket,
Hoping to shield myself from the mess within.

Self-sabotage seeps into my thoughts,
Diminishing the joy meant for me,
I find myself living for others, not myself,
Neglecting the fullness of life's embrace.

But I stand prepared to surrender,
To immerse myself in the golden warmth it
offers,
For within my basket's unwavering presence,
I find love and support, always there for me.

Within the realm of my basket, the sun's gentle
grasp,

I entrust my treasured moments to bask,
Yet lately, its radiant allure seems elusive,
As if denying me entry, leaving me passive.

How does it discern my rebellious intent,
As my mind echoes the sorrow my heart invents,
Seeking refuge, I turn to my sacred retreat,
Yearning for respite, a reprieve from defeat.

Self-sabotage weaves through my tangled
thoughts,
Distorting the enjoyment of life's tapestry
oughts,
For too long, I've lived to please those around
me,
Neglecting my own desires, in silence bound.

But now, I stand poised to savor the golden
embrace,
Eager to immerse in the warmth, without haste,
Within my basket's cradle, love and support
reside,
Ever present, devoted, a constant guide.

So, I unlock the gates, step forward with grace,
Embracing solace, letting joy find its rightful
place,
My basket, a sanctuary, a faithful friend,
Guiding me through shadows, until the end.

For within its woven confines, I discover anew,
The power to nourish, to heal, to pursue,
With each passing moment, its embrace grows,
Enveloping me in tranquility, as life unfolds.

Egocentric

In the realm of self, I find my pride,
Not in superiority, but in what resides,
For within me, a uniqueness unfolds,
A tapestry woven, a story untold.

I don't claim to be better than the rest,
But in this world, I am truly blessed,
For there exists no duplicate of my being,
A singular essence, infinitely freeing.

In the depths of self-awareness, I find,
A celebration of the soul, unconfined,
Embracing individuality, unapologetically,
Unveiling the treasures within, authentically.

To know there's none quite like me,
It ignites a flame, sets my spirit free,
For it grants me the power to shine,
To carve my path, a destiny divine.

Egocentric, some may perceive,
But it's the love for self, I believe,
A self-love that fuels compassion's fire,
Radiating strength, and empathy entire.

In this journey of self-discovery profound,
I navigate the depths where treasures abound,
Embracing my uniqueness, uncontained,
For it is in authenticity, I am sustained.

So, let me cherish the essence I possess,
Embrace the beauty of my distinct address,
For in celebrating my own worth and truth,
I cultivate a world of harmony and growth.

Deep Aurora

In the depths of my being, I find serenity,
A connection to the spirit, pure and free.
Harmonizing with the elements, earth, and sky,
The symphony of existence, resonating nearby.

As I close my eyes, a kaleidoscope unfurls,
Colors dancing behind lids, vibrant and twirled.
Each hue reveals the essence of my soul's flame,
An intricate tapestry, with no two shades the
same.

The deep aurora reflects my energy's core,
An inner radiance, like never seen before.
It shimmers and glows, in shades profound,
Unveiling the depths where my truth is found.

In this ethereal realm, my spirit takes flight,
Soaring through the cosmos, in boundless light.
I merge with the universe, in a cosmic embrace,
Embodying the oneness, with celestial grace.

Feeling centered, immersed in the cosmic flow,
A union with the universe, where secrets glow.
With each breath, I align with the sacred within,
An eternal dance, where my soul finds kin.

The deep aurora reveals my essence untamed,
A symphony of colors, where my energy is named.
In this sacred stillness, I find my truest state,
A radiant connection, where love and peace await.

The elements surround me, an orchestra of sublime,
Fire, water, air, and earth, in harmonious rhyme.
In the colors behind closed eyes, secrets come alive,
A universe within, where dreams and hopes revive.

The spectrum unfolds, revealing emotions deep and true,
Each shade tells a story, both old and anew.
In the deep aurora, I witness my soul's rebirth,
A journey inward, a rediscovery of my worth.

Love, A

As I pen these words, I envision you, smiling
brightly,
A testament to the journey, the battles you've
fought.
If by chance your smile has faded away,
Know that this too shall pass, a fleeting display.

This letter, my love, is for the brown girl in the
mirror,
With curls embracing the sky, defying any fear.
I want you to know, my dear reflection,
You've achieved what once seemed beyond
perception.

Proudly, you've marched through trials and
strife,
Conquering challenges, embodying the strength
of life.
From the depths of doubt, you emerged with
grace,
Living out your dreams, at your own pace.

No longer bound by limitations imposed,
You've discovered the path where your passion
flows.

Every step forward, a testament to your power,
Manifesting dreams, hour by dedicated hour.

Life has offered its share of hurdles and tests,
Yet, you've risen above, giving your very best.
With unwavering determination, you've soared,
Unlocking the doors to treasures yet unexplored.

Remember, my dear, this is just the beginning,
The journey unfolding, new chapters forever
spinning.
There's still much more to uncover and embrace,
A world of endless possibilities to chase.

You hold within you a reservoir of light,
Gifts and talents ready to shine ever so bright.
Embrace the limitless potential you possess,
For you have so much to offer, nothing less.

As you read these words, may they resonate,
A reminder of the strength you cultivate.
You must have faith in the dreams you pursue,
For in your heart lies a new universe.

Love,

A